Dorothy Porter's award-winning crime thriller in verse, *The Monkey's Mask*, has become a modern Australian classic. Her other verse novels include *Wild Surmise* and *What a Piece of Work*, both short-listed for the Miles Franklin Award, *Akhenaten* and *El Dorado*. She has written libretti and song lyrics and seven volumes of poetry, most recently *The Bee Hut*.

On Passion was completed just before her death in December 2008.

Writers in the *On Series*

Fleur Anderson
Gay Bilson
John Birmingham
Julian Burnside
Blanche d'Alpuget
Paul Daley
Robert Dessaix
Juliana Engberg
Sarah Ferguson
Nikki Gemmell
Stan Grant
Germaine Greer
Sarah Hanson-Young
Jonathan Holmes
Daisy Jeffrey
Susan Johnson
Malcolm Knox

Barrie Kosky
Sally McManus
David Malouf
Paula Matthewson
Katharine Murphy
Dorothy Porter
Leigh Sales
Mark Scott
Tory Shepherd
Tim Soutphommasane
David Speers
Natasha Stott Despoja
Anne Summers
Tony Wheeler
Ashleigh Wilson
Elisabeth Wynhausen

Dorothy Porter

On Passion

hachette
AUSTRALIA

Every attempt has been made to locate the copyright holders for
material quoted in this book. Any person or organisation that may
have been overlooked or misattributed may contact the publisher.

⊟ hachette
AUSTRALIA

Published in Australia and New Zealand in 2020
by Hachette Australia
(an imprint of Hachette Australia Pty Limited)
Level 17, 207 Kent Street, Sydney NSW 2000
www.hachette.com.au

First published in 2010 by Melbourne University Publishing

A catalogue record for this
book is available from the
National Library of Australia

NATIONAL
LIBRARY
OF AUSTRALIA

ISBN: 978 0 7336 4397 2 (paperback)

Original cover concept by Nada Backovic Design
Text design by Alice Graphics
Typeset by Typeskill
Printed and bound in Australia by McPherson's Printing Group

MIX
Paper from
responsible sources
FSC® C001695

The paper this book is printed on is certified against the
Forest Stewardship Council® Standards. McPherson's Printing
Group holds FSC® chain of custody certification SA-COC-005379
FSC® promotes environmentally responsible, socially beneficial
and economically viable management of the world's forests.

Survivor of the Auto da Fé

My first interesting poem was inspired by the Spanish Inquisition. It's a histrionic dramatic monologue in the voice of a heretic burning at the stake. The other character in the poem is a rat, accompanying the heretic to his (or her) agonising execution. The rat is the survivor of the poem and, when things get literally too hot, leaps from the clothes of the burning heretic to safety. The heretic keeps on sizzling in lonely betrayed agony. In a ghastly epiphany, he recognises the fleeing rat as the last of his religious faith. The heretic dies a broken sceptic.

I was seventeen, in my last year at school, and cheerfully morbid—no doubt in reaction to my own relatively peaceful middle-class childhood on Sydney's northern beaches. Ghoulishly, I wanted to know what it felt like being burnt to death in a public square to the howls of a righteous mob. I didn't know that the Inquisition, in its own twisted righteous logic, used fire not as a weapon of torture (or spectator sport) but as purification. My scorching new poem, 'Survivor of the Auto da Fé', was, unbeknown to me, a form of purification too.

I was raised an Anglican. But in Sydney the good old C of E has never been a laissez-faire tolerant form of respectable Christianity. Sydney Anglicanism snorts fire and brimstone. It has done so since its earliest days in the heathen colony, when the Reverend Samuel Marsden, nicknamed 'The Flogging Parson', beat his recalcitrant convicts with the cat-o'-nine-tails. Every summer for most of my adolescent school years, I got a pungent taste of Sydney Anglicanism at Camp Howard. And I relished it.

Camp Howard, based pretty much on the American religious summer-camp model, was a group of camps run by the Sydney Anglicans for secondary-school kids. They were very cheap, run by church volunteers—the mostly saintly 'counsellors' not long out of adolescence themselves—and were in beautiful locations. Some of the most boisterously happy experiences of my life were at Camp Howard. I loved the fresh mix of kids—many from 'rough' western-suburbs schools and backgrounds. These kids were wild, in the fairly innocent way of the mid-sixties, and a bracing tonic for my own private-school snobbery and gutlessness. Some of my favourite school buddies would come with me, and Camp Howard brought out the best wildness in them too. I spent much of my time in joyous mucking-up, protected by the safety net of wonderfully tolerant young adults.

The prime purpose of Camp Howard was not to give teenagers a chance to learn archery, paddle a canoe or earn their Bronze Medallion; it was to save their souls. My soul was saved at least ten times, sometimes in grand theatrical style. And when my human saviour was cute, my rapture for Jesus was even more intense.

With sophisticated hindsight, I appreciate now what heaven those camps were for a gay romantic. If only I'd had a boy-pal to swish about with and sigh over Jesus—and our crushes. Of course that sense of gay—'camp'—camaraderie was a thing of the distant future. But bless the sweet, blind innocence of those days: I got away with blue murder.

Yet by the time I wrote 'Survivor of the Auto da Fé', I had changed. I wrote the poem with a radio blasting rock music in my ear. It was 1971—the year after the deaths of my dark gods, Janis Joplin, Jim Morrison and Jimi Hendrix. Their daemonic songs were my new hymns, while their daemonic enchantment captivated me and made my pen fly. Their music Lit My Fire—the fire that now crackled so fiercely, with perverse energy and real freedom, in my new poem in which I play both the heretic's and the rat's roles. I flee the martyr's masochism into new life and survival, while I mourn the loss of faith— and the failure of love (another camp infatuation had hit the dust). But the poem ends with a true-believing Romantic's flourish, one that would make more than one cameo appearance in future poems. I make a stand for love. I make a stand for self-fuelling passion.

The poem was my first experience of the supernatural potency of poetry. My poetry knew more about me than I consciously knew about myself. It knew my secret self, its history and its likely future. Now when I read 'Survivor of the Auto da Fé' the hairs go up on my neck because, regardless of its obvious flaws, there is something eerily knowing and uncanny about it. I didn't know when writing it that my own Jewish ancestors were forced to flee the Spanish Inquisition to the sanctuary of Holland. Sometimes I feel the poem is channelling the voice of an ancestor who may well have gone through the experience the poem so gruesomely describes—with or without the rat. The poem at times soars above the very immature teenager who wrote it, and the imaginative black verve of it, achieved relatively effortlessly, I rarely achieved again. But when I did, it was with a gratitude to all my angels, demons and rats.

Survivor of the Auto da Fé

You can remember
   me
I am your charred
   conscience.

I lived in a village
  of bones and grey
    smoke.
From my dry, scratchy
    prison
I talked heresy
  with the rats.
I kissed one for
  love,
  his red, feasted little
    eyes
swore he were
  a fellow unbeliever.
He itched at his mangeing
    fur
  and clicked his teeth
    of Jesuits.

'Tomorrow I burn
        with you,'
his nails scraped
along the floor
like a chalk on a
        tombstone.

The morning was
    a Spanish gypsy
        in its colour of yellow
stinking flying skirts.
The rat gnawed at his
        own droppings.
'We'll burn well
    on such a
        morning.
Rain would have us
        sizzling.'

ON PASSION

I sunbaked in his
   wisdom.

The sun seeped like
   a clay pipe leaking
   through my prison's
     bars.
I kissed the collecting
     pool of yellow
  dust adios
  while stashing my
  religion between my
    breast and my black
     coffin cloak.

He became my hair
    shirt
   as he bit my flesh
   raw.

But I smiled from
   my chains
   when my earthly
      judges came.

I burnt as wildly
   as a guitar strum.
My smile withered first
   dropping as white ash
   to the faggots.
The rat ripped through
      my rags
   and blinked at my
      god-fearing audience.
He profaned to them,
   vomited on his paw
   only to return to
      my cloak,

anger chipping his
   teeth.

My pain had melted
   and dripped as fat
      to the flames.
My broiling brains
     declared me a martyr
       and I looked for
         Christ.
'He'll come,' rat
    scratched.
'He'll not forget,' rat
    bit.

The flames came stronger
   than Luther,
the wings of the rat's
    favourite flea

caught afire.

Was its high buzz

    a shriek of

        insect agony?

The rat went jaundice

    under his whiskers.

My rags glowed

    like Seville

when the red sun

    is impaled

on the cliff spire.

The rat felt the evil heat

    of my death

    and like St John's Gospel

        he leapt from my charcoal

        breast.

Gingerly
 through hissing
  orange and yellow
   godlings,
unscathed,
 except for a singed
  tail,
went my religion.

My stake branded
 my last breaths
 and I screamed,
'Father, revenge me!
Father, feed him
 to the cats
  of Tartarus!'

Rat, you live still
 and grow fat

in the holes of the
   Master's mansion.
My survivors, my
   wet-eyed weepers,
  my inheritors
feed you your
   nutrients.
I forgive the Jesuits,
  the ghouls of
    Virgin Mary's
    candle,
but you, rat, I
   will poison.
Beware of the sour
  milk pools
 you lap at.
They were tenderness

and shall be
    once more.
The love to singe
    your whiskers.

Dionysian daze

My first collection of poetry, *Little Hoodlum*, was published in 1975. I was twenty-one. Much of it was written in a trance of poetic intoxication, and many of the poems still drone The Flight of the Maenad Bee. The book is prefaced with a quote from Robert Graves' heterodox classic *The White Goddess*: 'The Night Mare is one of the cruellest aspects of the White Goddess'. (I still love the Goth overtones of that quote.)

While writing many of the poems in *Little Hoodlum*, I was studying— drinking neat—the work of the controversial philosopher Friedrich Nietzsche. His first book, *The Birth of Tragedy*, was an inspiration. Like Nietzsche, I was bedazzled by ancient Greek culture, especially dramatic poetry, and I loved the rumblings of paganism in its glorious prime. I too wanted to throw off the constricting shackles of 'tame' Christianity.

At roughly the same time I was devouring the poetry of adolescent, feral genius Arthur Rimbaud. But I had real problems with the 'derangement of the senses' dictum: I simply wasn't brave or reckless enough to lurch down that dangerous path. In reality I wasn't a hallucinating,

self-destructive male poet writing passion-
ate poetry; rather, I was a physically timid,
overtly cautious, imaginative woman writ-
ing passionate poetry—for which I relied
on my own sweet drug of addiction:
romantic love.

I also had a good friend in Dionysian
instruction: the last of the great Athenian
dramatic poets, Euripides, who accord-
ing to Nietzsche's scornful denunciation
in *The Birth of Tragedy*, ruined and gutted
the Dionysian music of true tragic poetry
forever. I disagreed as a young university
student and training-wheels poet, and I
disagree now. Despite Nietzsche's preju-
dice, I believe Euripides shows the great-
est and grimmest understanding of the
Dionysian: the intoxicating and the most

dangerously sacred and direct experience of mystical truth. He shows how to respect and live with it. He shows what happens in graphic, unsparing detail if you respect it too little or live with it too much. Maybe Nietzsche is right in accusing Euripides of being just another mask for that manipulative nihilist Socrates, who Nietzsche believes routed classical Hellenism in all its glittering glory. Euripides is a strange voice indeed, a voice of magnificent poetry and hard-won moderation.

It was Euripides' *The Bacchae* that illuminated for me the fizz and fall of my own generation's headlong excess in the sixties and seventies. Euripides warns us that dreamy, hippy Woodstock will not so gradually nor so prettily morph into violent, bikie Altamont. Those of us who were then so rapturously made of Joni's Woodstock soaring-star stuff would not much more than a year later be huddling behind futile Mick pleading 'Gimme Shelter', as he begged the Hells Angels to stop stabbing the punters.

Moderation was not something I embraced with Delphic calm, but rather something I gutlessly and gracelessly caved in to. Often at parties, when the drugs appeared, I felt like Euripides' doomed wowser King Pentheus among the berserk Maenads. A few puffs of dope would relax me; more would befuddle me and let nightmares leak in. On one memorable occasion around a fire in Tasmania I mixed wine and dope, and slowly a real terror crept over me. I imagined myself trapped in a phone booth during the 1967 fires. I imagined myself trapped and burning to death. I have been excruciatingly careful with drugs ever since. Perhaps Euripides would approve.

When Agauë, still in the Dionysian trance, presents her own father, Cadmus, with the wrenched-off head of Pentheus, she believes she is presenting a kill. She stands drenched in the gore of her son and says with pride:

> I have left weaving at the loom for
>> greater things,
> For hunting wild beasts with my bare
>> hands. See this prize,

Here in my arms; I won it, and it shall
    be hung
On your palace wall.

Agaüe is in for a rude shock, and we
know and wait for it to come. There's no
avoiding the lesson: gorging on the Dark
Mysteries brings terrible consequences.
But if we totally eschew them we become
Pentheus: withered, moralising, soul-dead
and doomed. Euripides acknowledges that
living is no cinch. And the gods, whether
they exist or not, amuse themselves at our
fragile expense while insisting we worship
and respect them. Euripides did little to
enhance the reputation of religion, and
paid a heavy price for it. Both he and his

plays were condemned as gloomy and impious. Rumour had it that after his exile to the Macedonian court he was torn to pieces by a pack of offended Maenads. The young and spiky Nietzsche of *The Birth of Tragedy* would no doubt have approved of such a fitting Orphic end for the poet who killed classical tragedy, though his own death from tertiary syphilis in a mental asylum shrieks a Dionysian warning straight from Euripides.

Great Pan is dead!

One of the most poignant passages in *The Birth of Tragedy*, whether historically true or not, is, as far as I'm concerned, far more dreadful than Nietzsche's later, more famous pronouncement that God is dead: 'the Greek sailors in the time of Tiberius heard from a lonely island the agonising cry "Great Pan is dead!"'

There can be no worse news if Pan, the hairy, goat-legged god of Nature, is really dead. It means Nature itself is sterile, and, if not dead, dying. One of Pan's most visible attributes is his massive erect phallus. He represents the natural world at its most earthy and essential. He is also the incarnation of an untamed erotic creativity as he plays his pipes. I have always wanted to hear his music and have it play through my poetry.

Music has been my draught of intoxication since the very moment I first heard The Beatles in early 1964. It was just before my tenth birthday and I was sitting in a hot car outside Manly Hospital. My parents were visiting my younger sister, Mary, who the previous week had been seriously mauled by a bulldog. It was a horrible time—not helped by the hospital bureaucracy banning children under fourteen from visiting the wards. I was anxious and bored, trying to amuse my three-year-old youngest sister, so I clicked on the car radio. And I heard a sound that changed my brain chemistry and my life forever: the opening chords of 'I Wanna Hold Your Hand'. I have been a Beatles pop/rock music maniac ever since, and have written virtually all my poems to rock riffs and rhythm—the catchier, the darker, the louder, the gutsier the better. Whatever works. Music has been my magic. I have no idea how and why it works on my heart, imagination and pen the way it does, although Nietzsche has given me a clue in my recent re-reading of *The Birth of Tragedy*. He refers to the German poet Schiller's method of composition:

> Schiller confessed that, prior to composing, he experienced not a logically connected series of images but rather a *musical mood*. 'With me emotion is at the beginning without clear and definite ideas; those ideas do not arise until later on. A certain musical disposition of mind comes first, and after follows the poetical idea'.

I don't know whether Schiller had a trick to bring on his musical mood. Mine is simple: I inject my psychic veins with music. In my teens I was threaded to my tinny, tiny transistor. Now I'm spoilt rotten with my favourite invention of all time: my spell-box iPod.

I am frequently asked, of all the poems I have ever read and loved, which is my all-time favourite. It's one of those frustrating questions for which there are a million shifting possible answers. Nevertheless, I do have a poem that has marked me for life: 'The God Abandons Antony' by the twentieth-century Greek poet CP Cavafy. It's strikingly unusual in both perspective and tone. Rather than have Antony describe in a traditional dramatic monologue the mire in which he and his lover Cleopatra are drowning, this is a post-passion, paying-the-piper poem, with a Kiplingesque voice of stoical instruction:

As one long prepared, and full of
　　courage,
as is right for you who were given this
　　kind of city,
go firmly to the window
and listen with deep emotion,
but not with the whining, the pleas of a
　　coward;
listen—your final pleasure—to the
　　voices,
to the exquisite music of that strange
　　procession,
and say goodbye to her, to the
　　Alexandria you are losing.

There's a terrible double whammy in this poem. As you read it, you feel all the joy, grace and wild good fortune that only divine blessing can bestow draining out of it. You, the sober reader, struggle to hear the last strains of the 'exquisite music' as the silent darkness closes around the utterly solitary figure of Antony. Great Pan is not dead; he's just leaving forever. There's a profound, sophisticated wisdom here, and it's eerily comforting.

> Above all, don't fool yourself, don't say
> it was a dream, your ears deceived you:
> don't degrade yourself with empty
>   hopes like these.
> As one long prepared, and full of
>   courage,

as is right for you who were given this
    kind of city,
go firmly to the window ...

In other words: no whingeing. Everything glorious, from cities to music, is a gift. But the one thing that is absolutely yours is courage, even the courage to watch the gods leave, taking their music with them.

I have a very superstitious relationship with the poems I love. I carry 'The God Abandons Antony' within me like a talisman to temper my grinding fear of losing my own 'music', along with the hope that I will accept with stoical grace the time when, inevitably, I too am just a parched empty vessel.

The god Pan is the spirit of fecundity in wild nature, in sexual potency and in undiluted joyous creativity. He is rampantly pagan and unchristian. I believe that Christianity killed something in poetry, put lead in its step and muffled its wildest music. When I listen to my favourite rock music, from Tina Turner growling drug-fucked temptation in 'Acid Queen' through Bruce Springsteen's blistering 'She's the One' to Jimi Hendrix's guitar sketching murder and misery in 'Hey Joe', I hear a dark energy I want to tap into and flood through my poetry. The blistering subterranean pipes of Pan?

The blues singer Robert Johnson made a notorious pact with the Devil at the crossroads so he could truly play the

Devil's tunes. The Devil is of course just timorous Christian doublespeak for Pan. Would I go 'to the crossroads' and '[fall] down on my knees' like Johnson did? Or was there a moment, a meeting, with Pan I have missed? Or is this primeval dare still ahead of me?

The magic of snakes

I dedicated my last verse novel, *El Dorado*, to 'the magic of snakes'. During much of the time I was writing the book I was very ill, and then, thankfully, in healing remission from cancer. The dedication was not only gut-felt gratitude to the traditional emblem of the doctor's art, but also my own private acknowledgement of an ancient holy symbol. And much more than a mere symbol. Real and living snakes are sacred to me. They are the nub of my own idiosyncratic pantheism.

When Arthur Evans was excavating the palace at Knossos on the island of Crete, he kept unearthing extraordinary statuettes of bare-breasted priestesses whose arms were swathed in wriggling snakes. It became clear that the snake was a revered and key element in Minoan worship. There was also something potently feminine about the Minoan cult of the snake—nothing like the debased and diabolical serpent-demon of the Judaeo-Christian Garden of Eden, which is typically represented as a penis-headed tempter of the shallow, disobedient moron Eve. Minoan snakes command awe, yet are on thrillingly intimate terms with their female handlers, whether goddesses or human priestesses. There is an electric connection between the chthonic energy of the writhing snake and human religious ritual. And no fear, revulsion or anthropomorphic caricature.

Yes, I know I sound like an anachronistic seventies lesbian Goddess-worshipping feminist bending cultural anthropology to her own wishful-thinking purpose. So be it. Sneer away. Snakes are sacred to me too. And I regard it as a profound blessing every time I'm lucky enough to catch a swishing-tailed glimpse of one in the wild, even as I keep my distance. Though, I confess, I took off like a rocket when a territorial king brown snake in Central Australia suddenly reared up out of a ditch and came straight for me. I didn't linger to test whether he was more frightened of me than I was of him, as popular wisdom would have it. King browns can move like lightning and I got the shock of my life.

Many core Aboriginal Dreaming stories are about snakes, such as that of the great Rainbow Serpent, or the violent battle between a female python and a male brown snake at the birth of Uluru. After I was chased by the king brown, which was unfortunately then shot by the owner of the property where I was staying, riven with guilt, I bought a snake painting in Alice as some kind of reparation. Some years later I recognised that the snake in my painting was the python of Uluru protecting her eggs from the intruder brown snake. I don't know what this means. Am I off the hook or not?

There is a wonderful poem, 'Snake', by DH Lawrence, a mesmerising narrative of the simple act of watching a golden snake drinking from a water trough on a hot morning in Italy. Lawrence himself is intensely present, but without the verbal bloated machismo of too many of his poems, or the nature gush in his novels. This is passionate poetry—without embarrassing orgasmic seizures. Lawrence exalts the snake as a beautiful animal, but also recognises it to be poisonous, and finally, with reluctance, he throws 'a clumsy log' at it. The snake 'Writhed like lightning, and was gone'. Almost immediately Lawrence regrets his 'mean act'.

The visitation of the snake was a blessing, a sacred event, and Lawrence's own fear and 'pettiness' have spoilt it. I think Lawrence, for once, might have been too tough on himself. I have read this poem many times over many years, and every time I'm left with a vision of the lovely snake drinking while the poet tenderly watches. That Italian morning is now a part of my own life. I hardly ever remember that Lawrence scared the snake away.

Snakes have a habit of crawling into my poems too. I've even written a poem, 'Snake Story', with a rapturous tone about the death adder—a deadly snake notorious for its sloth, and thus easily stepped on. Whenever my sisters and I collected firewood for a bush barbecue, my father was always emphatic in his warnings about treading on a death adder, let alone picking one up by mistake. I still shudder when I remember the unusually large black adder dozing on the rock by the mountain creek in which we kids had just swum. My father bashed it to death with a stick. I thoroughly approved of his action at the time.

'Snake Story', written years later, now reads like a very strange, even disturbing, invocation—or perhaps another atonement to the rustling serpentine underground realm that continues to frighten and fascinate me.

Death adder,
will I ever learn
when to step on you?

Pluck out his eyes

In these paedophile-paranoid times there is nothing more heinous than to be caught downloading pornographic images of children. As one cyber-policeman graphically put it, those who delude themselves into believing that 'just looking' is harmless are in reality looking at and getting off on a vile crime scene. No one would argue with that. Men caught with these images become instant social outcasts everywhere, even in prison, where they're placed in protective custody from the rest of the prison community. It is no wonder that so many exposed paedophiles attempt suicide in the public shaming and black stink of their ruined lives.

But why is it perfectly legal to download, presumably in order to enjoy, images of violence and cruelty? As long as underage children are not involved it is pretty much open slather. How many hits do the websites boasting explicit scenes of terrorist beheadings receive? How many millions of images of gross cruelty to men, women or poor benighted animals are available for instant Googling? I have a weak stomach, and a visceral horror of cruelty—especially to animals. I don't dare look, because I know what I see will burn into my soul's retina forever.

Yet am I really free of this passion for cruelty? Even as I pat my cat and eat my vegetarian lunch?

For me there is one singularly unforgettable scene in Shakespeare. If you're game, turn to act 3, scene 7, Gloucester's castle in *King Lear*. You will witness—graphically on the page, let alone in performance—the taunting torture of an old man, the helpless and betrayed Gloucester.

'Pluck out his eyes', Goneril suggests, but leaves the actual blinding to her charming sister, Regan, and Regan's thug husband, Cornwall. With lashings of verbal relish, this pair of aristocratic monsters takes out, slowly, each of Gloucester's eyes. Cornwall, albeit now wounded by an appalled servant loyal to Gloucester, rams the atrocity home in one of Shakespeare's most indelible images: 'Out vile jelly! Where is thy lustre now?'

Why, even as my soul squirms, do I keep returning to this scene? Is the charge of physical and moral revulsion simply another way of feeling more intensely alive? What was Shakespeare feeling as he wrote it? Perhaps it was written in cynical cold blood to keep the theatre punters entertained. After all, Shakespeare was in direct competition with the bear-baiting garden around the corner—or the latest hanging, cutting, drawing and quartering of a traitor in the public square. Spectacles of blood and suffering were diverting to Elizabethan audiences, probably because their own lives were short, hard and perilous. What's my excuse, mired in safe modern middle-class comfort?

I have only once in my life hurt a fellow sentient creature for fun. It was back in my pre-adolescence, not a particularly sensitive time of my life, on a bushwalk in the Blue Mountains with my family and some old friends. We were having a barbecue by the creek, a beautiful mountain creek, cold and clear with rock pools. We used our chop bones to fish for the mysterious black crayfish, waving their claws from the rippled, sandy bottom. Mostly they were too smart for us, but the ones we pulled out, with the encouragement of my kindly naturalist parents, we would quickly let back in the water. There is no way I could have boiled one of those feisty animals alive. So why did I instead turn my restless, cruel attention on a shadowy blob of a tadpole? My friend Mick and I spent a good twenty minutes trying to shoot one in a shallow rock pool with a crude bow and arrow, rather foolishly made for us by my father. Despite my lifelong lack of eye–hand co-ordination, I finally succeeded. And the torn blob floated to the surface of the no-longer pristine water with its grey guts streaming. The game stopped. I can still remember my hot flush of self-disgust. There was no pleasure or glory in this kill at all. It made me feel less alive, as if I'd taken something away and left a horrible, senseless, ugly nothing in its place.

Are cruelty and violence more palatable, more exciting, when dressed up as scorching poetry in the mouths of mythic characters? Or does Shakespeare's art present, unblinkingly, the torture of an old man with such a gut-wrenching humanity that makes it different from, and in absolute and forever opposition to, the heartless, obscene banality of the real-life torture scenes on the Internet?

Finally, on the subject of cruelty, it is not necessarily those with the most passionate voices who have been most effective in confronting it and stopping it. When I was in my mid-twenties I read *Animal Liberation* by the philosopher Peter Singer. This book changed my life by changing my behaviour, as it did for thousands of others. Not only did I become a vegetarian, but henceforth I looked at the world differently. I became convinced that the human animal is not the centre of creation, and has no god-given right to behave blithely as if it is.

Peter Singer does not write about animals with the pulsing imagination of a DH Lawrence. Rather he writes like a dry atheist: his argument for animal rights is one of rationalism, logic and uncompromising conviction. But his work has had, arguably, more influence and has inspired more passionate activism than the work of any philosopher since Karl Marx.

The impossible

I have a passion for astrobiology. This is the most theoretical branch of biology since not one single solitary extraterrestrial organism has yet been discovered (fingers crossed for the *Phoenix* lander, digging in the Martian arctic soil as I type). I love the whole notion of astrobiology because it is brazenly optimistic. It rests on the belief that there is life elsewhere, and we Earthlings may be forced one day to embrace life forms, even alien civilisations, that now seem fanciful—if not impossible.

Everywhere an exciting but daunting sense of the impossible is permeating us all. Even in one's own chosen field, it is now impossible to know a fraction of the new information that is expanding at the speed of light. Sometimes, after cracking open my latest *New Scientist* magazine,

I have a crippling sense of vertigo. I feel worse than ignorant. I feel like I'm losing my grip on my own world. And yet I love living in these amphetamine-rush times.

I have decided to concentrate my thirst for new knowledge on the latest discoveries in astronomy. These are happening so fast, so spectacularly, that I struggle to understand the basics, let alone keep up. But my curiosity remains at fever pitch. I want to know about the new planets being spotted orbiting alien suns and red dwarfs. The hunt is on for planets like our own Earth, rocky and with signs of liquid water, in what is called the Goldilocks Zone—not too hot and not too cold. It is impossible to anticipate what we will discover on these planets. Strange geological phenomena? Bizarre life forms? No one knows. Already exploration in our own solar system has yielded images of landscapes, like the volcanoes on Jupiter's fiery moon Io, and the recently discovered ice geysers of Saturn's moon Enceladus, which no one had guessed were there.

I'm astonished that very few of my fellow writers, apart from the science-fiction community, share my passion for this extraordinary human adventure into space. I have no doubt that if John Donne were writing his metaphysical poetry today he'd be as mad with excitement for this fresh treasure-trove of knowledge and imagery as I am. The astronomers I have been fortunate enough to meet have been among the happiest and most energised people I have ever known. Their work is literally wondrous.

Notions of the impossible have, unfortunately, also been gatekeepers—and shackles. Especially for women. Patriarchal orthodox religion, whether Hindu, Muslim, Jewish or Christian, has offered dreams of possibility, in either the physical or spiritual realm, to men only. Any woman who embraces the shabby equal-but-different deal offered by the Holy Fathers of any of these faiths is, at best, a deluded mug and, at worst, a scourge and gaoler of other women. It is only in the very recent past that possibilities for women have expanded—and then, mainly in the West. But in the last twenty years or so, fundamentalism of all creeds has dragged women back. The failure of communism, or socialism in its more acceptable guise, was a global disaster, I believe, for the advancement of women. The vacuum it left has been insidiously filled with ancient prejudices, traditional superstitions and the old religious fungus.

Arthur Rimbaud in his sulphurous prose poem 'A Season in Hell' has a section titled 'The Impossible'. He goads his own flailing, disillusioned spirit: 'My spirit, take care. No violent decisions about salvation. Start working!—Ah! science does not move fast enough for us!'

No, science does not work fast enough. It can create problems as it solves them.

It can be ethically fraught. In the wrong hands—the military establishment or the ambitiously amoral or simply the unimaginative—it can be a foul, destructive monster. Yet as a twenty-first-century feminist, I am inclined, with vigilant caution, to trust it with my freedom and wellbeing, rather than be walled up again by traditional religion. And, who knows, science in the right hands may lead us to some alluring bold inventive impossible.

Nelly, I am Heathcliff

Brooding from the reflective fastness of middle age, I wonder if some of the most deeply passionate experiences of my life have happened between the covers of a book. Much of my own poetry, in and out of the disguises of my verse novels, has focused with all the intensity I could muster on erotic love. Some of this has been garnered from my own life experience— I was about to add the offhandedly modern 'of course'. 'Of course' nothing. The most scorching novel in the English language, *Wuthering Heights*, was written by a reclusive clergyman's daughter, Emily Brontë, who spent most of her time doing household chores or wandering the moors beyond the Haworth parsonage.

The sketchy details of Brontë's life have been forensically scrutinised, in the more than a hundred and fifty years since her early death from consumption, for the faintest evidence of a secret love life. Somerset Maugham, in an entertaining and insightful essay on Brontë's life and work, speculates with his familiar worldly cynicism that Brontë may simply have suffered a disastrous love affair at boarding school—and then fed off it for the rest of her life. This speculation is not quite as silly as it sounds. Brontë rarely ventured from her home, and one of the few occasions when she did was to go to school. She left her school suddenly and prematurely, in mysteriously unhappy circumstances.

The usual explanation is that Brontë was homesick, almost pathologically so. But it is difficult to believe that Brontë was such a sook. Her family nickname was 'the Major'. She was physically tough and fearless. She dressed oddly and whistled like a man, and she showed no romantic interest in men whatsoever. Maybe Maugham isn't totally barking up the wrong tree. But no psychological guesswork about its enigmatic author explains the nuclear force of *Wuthering Heights*. And nothing else ever written touches it.

There is, paradoxically, much more convincing grown-up sex in Jane Austen than in Emily Brontë. Heathcliff and Cathy never consummate their mutual passion for each other. Their most intimate moment is when Heathcliff digs up then wraps himself around Cathy's fresh corpse. This scene could so easily have degenerated into the ghoulish farce of the Gothic novels that Brontë and all her writer siblings devoured as kids. It doesn't. It splinters your bones and shivers your heart even as its likelihood in the real world, apart from criminal perversity, is negligible, laughable.

Emily Brontë is writing about a kind of passion beyond most human experience. Perhaps just as well. She describes feelings that are all-consuming and totally destructive. Yet there is some cavernous emptiness in the reader of *Wuthering Heights* that longs to be filled—ravished— by these feelings. Their musical accompaniment is Isolde's orgasmic swan song in Wagner's *Tristan and Isolde*.

Frankly, I have always envied Cathy and Heathcliff, especially their reunited ghosts wandering forever the nocturnal Yorkshire moors. I know only too well how utterly claustrophobic and toxic is the line: 'Nelly, I *am* Heathcliff'. I know that real and live-able and enduring love is not a frenzied cannibal's feast. But how intoxicating the dream of a passion that defiantly trounces everything—even death. Where did Emily Brontë find it?

Stuffed in the mouths of mummified crocodiles

The ancient maestro of the lyric love poem was a small, dark-haired woman called Sappho, born on the island of Lesbos, in roughly 612 BCE. Her poems in Aeolian Greek were sung or recited accompanied by a lyre, hence the musical origin for the term *lyrical poetry*. It's not known whether Sappho herself wrote her poems down—but her fans did. Her poems were copiously copied and performed by professional singers all over the Greek world. In her own time she was famous, much like a modern internationally celebrated singer-songwriter such as Joni Mitchell. But more so. Sappho's talent was lauded for hundreds of years after her death as extraordinary to the point of freakish. She composed and performed in a belligerently religious man's world, where artistic gifts were treated with awe and believed to come directly from the gods. What did it mean when the gods so favoured a rather plain woman?

I own a number of translations of Sappho. My favourite has remained the Shambhala Pocket Classic by Mary Barnard. It fits in the palm of my hand, and I have tucked it lovingly into my backpack for most of my travels. There are few joys equal to reading a Sappho fragment—and that's mostly what they are—first thing in the morning. The poems, in these lovely and distilled translations by Barnard, jump across the gap of over two and a half thousand years and feel quiveringly fresh. No poet embodies Ezra Pound's dictum 'Only emotion endures' like Sappho. She feeds you ambrosial honey one minute, bitter bilious heartbreak the next.

Sappho virtually invented what is now the most enduring and popular poetry— the love song. It is a nonsense to say that poetry is dead, dying or only read by a few constipated poetasters mostly interested in their own self-indulgent ramblings. The love song, good, bad or indifferent, blasts or seeps from the field, the street, the shower, the theatre, the radio, the television, the computer and the iPod all over the world. The oral love lyric is, hands down, the dominant creative use of language in human history. Its only rival is the religious hymn—and Sappho was a deft hand at writing those as well.

Sappho was simply the first Western poet to speak in beautifully lucid ordinary words about her own emotions:

Day in, day out

I hunger and
I struggle

She hungers and struggles with loneliness, with her fears of ageing and death, with a rival stealing a lover, with her impatience for the presence of a beloved face. Most passionately, she hungers and struggles with capricious Aphrodite, the 'snare-knitter' goddess of love, who floods her with blessings—or torments her with deaf ears. Everything Sappho writes, even if written in jealous rage, glistens with 'delicious dew'. The thrill of reading her in the original has been raved about by the dustiest of classical scholars.

Her most famous poem expresses for all time the almost medical symptoms of stifled erotic passion:

> a thin flame runs under
> my skin …
>
> and I turn paler than
> dry grass. At such times
> death isn't far from me

The world owes the preservation of this boiling geyser of a poem to a translation by the Latin poet Catullus, a thermal spring himself and an ardent admirer of Sappho.

There is something radioactive about the work of Sappho. Each burning word seems to have a half-life of thousands of years. Yet we have so little of it: only the odd word or phrase survives from many lost poems. Some of what we have was found quoted in ancient grammar books, or in a mention or translation by a fellow poet hundreds of years after Sappho's death. The most bizarre and tantalising discoveries have been uncovered in the dry air of the Egyptian desert on discarded papyrus: fragments of Sappho have been found torn into strips and stuffed into the mouths of mummified crocodiles.

In 2005, to delirious excitement from Sappho readers, a new and complete poem was pieced together from cloth pasted around a human mummy. In it, Sappho laments the loss of her 'tender young body' and curses the physical pains of growing old. The poet's hair is whitening and her knees are giving out. Alas, it made a lot of grim sense to me. I hope the next poem discovered will be more joyful. Sappho back! And on delicious song.

How lovely to be eleven years old and greedy!

Agatha Christie, in a foreword to a collection of stories including her personal favourite, 'The Adventure of the Christmas Pudding', revels in memories of her childhood Christmases, especially the endless courses of lethally rich food. Her foreword has an unselfconscious jollity and nostalgia that now reads as awkwardly as a waddling guileless dodo. And just as extinct.

It's now fashionable to publicly wring one's wan, wretched hands over an unhappy—better still, abusive—childhood. My generation, unlike our buttoned-up parents, has become perhaps rather too comfortable with retrospective whingeing—and with too much therapy. Have we lost our childhood gusto? Do we all need a good dunking in Enid Blyton's famous 'lashings of lemonade'? No—we wouldn't risk it: the devil, diabetes, might get us.

I'm with Agatha. I treasure my lovely greedy moments, whether from childhood memories or, preferable by far, in the adult here and now. There is a Rabelaisian rhythm, a flavoursome swing to living that is being discounted or treated with moral distrust. I hate the new wowserism with its draconian measures to find and force down our throats the secret formula to eternal healthy life. My life sound-track still has the volume on high for Liza Minnelli's wistful 'Life is a cabaret, old chum. Come to the cabaret.' It beats the hell out of 'Come to the endless temper-ance meeting'.

In Homer, it's better to be alive than dead. In both *The Iliad* and *The Odyssey*, the underworld is no celestial paradise; it is a place of grey shadows and fam-ished ghosts who long for the smell, taste and touch of earthly pleasures again.

My closest experience to that of being a Homeric ghost was in the days following my cancer diagnosis when I looked at the world through a sickly grey gauze of envy. I envied the simple pleasures of good health and good appetite: a kid walking down the street eating an ice-cream; someone at the lights singing in their car; friends greeting each other outside a café; the swing of a healthy lean arrogant young man's arms; a lone diner dribbling a fat greasy burger. Oh God how I envied the well. I thought that anyone who didn't have cancer should be dancing joyously down the street like Gene Kelly in *Singing in the Rain*. And when I was finally well again, I never quite lost my immediate sense of ravenous gratitude.

One day I will die. One day I will not wake up to the smell of my partner bringing my morning mug of strong coffee up the stairs. One day I will be dust. But I have learnt the truly hard way that the passion I most cling to and ardently believe in is plain gusto. To respectfully paraphrase Christie—whose books were wonderful comfort and company when I was on chemo—how lovely to be fifty-four years old and greedy!

As kingfishers catch fire

One of the most beautiful things I have ever seen is an azure kingfisher fishing in a mangrove swamp near my family home in Pittwater, Sydney. I was paddling a canoe down a creek in a rare meditative silence (one of the joys of canoeing), when there was a sudden flash of orange/blue, like a jewelled dart suddenly spearing into the water. And as Gerard Manley Hopkins so exquisitely says, I watched a kingfisher 'catch fire'. In the same sonnet, Hopkins proclaims the unique wonder of 'each mortal thing': '*What I do is me: for that I came.*'

The italics belong to Hopkins. There is no poet in English less frightened of going overboard, of pushing language as hard as it will go into ecstasy—or despair. He is also, in my grateful opinion, the patron saint of birdwatchers.

Birdwatching is a passion of mine—yet another legacy from my naturalist parents. But unfortunately, birdwatching for some has become just another form of competition—and fanatical list-making.

I had a particularly unpleasant experience, in a small boat rocking on the rough water outside Sydney Harbour, with a group of young male birders obsessed with sighting and counting off trophy marine birds, especially albatrosses, which revel in high winds. The captain was a megalomaniac, too busy with his lists and binoculars to notice everyone vomiting around him. After a time I was so seasick and miserable that I wouldn't have noticed or cared if a Jurassic pterodactyl had flapped into view.

I hope in another life to go birdwatching with Hopkins. It is very hard to explain to the mocking non-enthusiast the thrill of watching a bird in the wild; even a flock of rainbow lorikeets streaking across a city park can make my heart race. Hopkins puts this sense of a gift, a rapturous epiphany, perfectly in 'The Windhover':

> … My heart in hiding
> Stirred for a bird …

These lines recall the first time I heard a lyrebird. I was walking in a rainforest mountain glen when suddenly I was caught by an extraordinary sound. I lay in wait for the bird to appear, in thrall to this remarkable mimic performing everything from a cockatoo to a lawn mower. Birdwatching can slow time, as each moment fills with something precious outside of one's self. For me, birdwatching is, without exaggeration, a religious experience. In 'God's Grandeur' Hopkins concludes his electrifying poem with the image of the Holy Ghost brooding 'with warm breast and with ah! bright wings' over the world like a maternal dove. It is an image ripe with biblical reference, but also dazzling with pantheistic echoes.

Birds have represented the realm of the sacred for much longer than Hopkins' personal faith of Catholicism has existed. Both the Egyptians and the Greeks believed that the spirits of the dead could return as birds. What a lovely idea. My partner feels the spirit of her dead father close when she sees a white-faced heron fishing in the rapids of Dights Falls. Perhaps, after my death, I will return to squawk with raucous glee and abandon over the heads of those I love in the guise of my totem bird, the sulphur-crested cockatoo.

Literary history now cages Hopkins in the depression and anguish of his despair sonnets, where in one poem he indelibly cries, 'No worst, there is none'. In another, he writes 'dead letters' to 'dearest him that lives alas! away'. This is not my Hopkins, the poet who, like his kingfisher, so often catches fire.

When he was dying his last words were 'I am happy, so happy'. What was he seeing? What beautiful free bird was he becoming?

Ravish me

Many years ago I wrote a very silly poem in the voice of a gay man on the nocturnal prowl. It was written with sincere envy. I have often said that in my next life I want to be a gay man—with the option of a time machine so I could travel with confidence and insouciance to the Athens of Plato's *Symposium* or the effete and witty cloisters of 1920s Oxbridge or the flesh-market Fire Island disco parties of the reckless 1970s. Simply, I have always envied gay sexual freedom, despite the repression, despite the times when the Piper was paid with AIDS. I am so sick of being a cautious and frequently frightened woman. It's a brake on a passionate life, and it's an ever-vigilant bore.

Alas, my yearning-to-be-a-gay-man poem just added its own flightless failure to the truth of Oscar Wilde's disdain for sincerity in art. But the poem did give me some honest information about what I'm mesmerised by in homoerotic life—and its art.

The key lies in the lightning-struck couplet that concludes a sonnet written to his God by one of literature's most famous heterosexual poets, John Donne. He was renowned for his wondrously witty and erotic love poetry to the woman he would later marry, but in his Holy Sonnets, written after he took holy orders, his lust of the spirit blows hotter than ever did his lust of the flesh. In Holy Sonnet XIV, 'Batter my heart, three person'd God', Donne pleads for God to overcome his resistance, as if Donne's soul were a trembling but eager virgin on her wedding night, and enter him by force if necessary. Donne, to put it crudely, begs God to rape him:

> Except you'enthral mee, never shall be
>   free,
> Nor ever chast, except you ravish mee.

I know these lines off by heart. They're some of the most indelibly erotic lines ever written. And they're unabashedly homo-erotic. God is a dominant male. Donne, in modern gay parlance, is a 'bottom'.

Almost the exact same sentiments are echoed in an uncompromisingly porno-graphic poem by the openly gay modern poet Allen Ginsberg, in his rhythmic groan of a poem 'Please Master':

> please master drive me thy vehicle,
>> body of love drops, sweat fuck
> body of tenderness, Give me your dog
>> fuck faster
> please master make me go moan on the
>> table …

If any poem has convinced me of the power of language to shock, indeed turn on a live audience, it is this one. I read it once, with shaking knees, to a festival crowd come to hear a discussion of erotic writing. Ginsberg, bless him, gave them more than they bargained for. And I got more than I bargained for too. One member of the audience—a complete stranger and, as far as I could tell, not a lesbian—told me that listening to me read the poem made her 'wet'. While on the other hand, four members of the audience conspicuously walked out during my reading, even though I had prefaced the poem with a triple-X warning.

What if instead of me (a middle-aged woman) an anonymous young Adonis had marched to the stage and read out not Ginsberg, but Donne's 'Batter my heart' as a yowl of homoerotic desire, a plea for sexual violation by a stronger, older man? I reckon 'ravish me' in his voice, suddenly cut free of the literary encrustations of centuries, would have melted lead—and wetted more than one pair of panties.

Camille Paglia, who describes herself as a sixties-style libertarian, and calls her provocative personal philosophy 'drag-queen feminism', makes a call to arms against bourgeois puritanism. She champions the bold and radical and sexy in the arts and culture, from the poetry of Allen Ginsberg to the guitar riffs of Keith Richards. She loathes political correctness and gentility. Even though she is in a long-term lesbian relationship herself, she is savage about the lesbian scene and lesbian culture (the latter she'd call an oxymoron). Paglia rhapsodises about a certain type of gay man—the same witty, cosmopolitan, cultured-to-his-fingertips sexual outlaw that I have romanticised in my restless female imagination as well.

Both Paglia and I were tomboys when we were kids. She dressed up as the toreador from *Carmen* (my favourite opera too), while I prowled around in my black ninja suit. Paglia's childhood was largely in the fifties; mine straddled the late fifties and the mid-sixties. Neither the fifties nor the early sixties were a great time to be a spirited little girl. It wasn't just in Paglia's and my twisted envious imaginations that boys were having most of the fun—they were. Except of course if the boy was gay, and then his life was an unadulterated nightmare. It was far easier to be a tomboy than a sissy.

Both Paglia and I like men. I have had close male friends all my life. My male friends have been a sweet refuge from the turbulence of my romantic life with women. I agree heartily with Paglia that sexual segregation, whether in straight or gay circles, is poison to both sexes. And after a lifetime of oscillation and muddle I now know that for me sexual passion is bisexual. Or, simply, I like what's sexually exciting and ravishing, whether in spectacle—like many lesbians, I have enjoyed gay porn (it sure ain't faked)—or in the realm of my own imagination where I want to find and deliver scenarios, characters and poems that are magnetic with sexual energy. Dream on, you may well be sniggering—especially my fellow writers. And for a gutless moment let me join you. But how many readers have we lost because we have ignored the ancient silent cry: ravish me.

I burnt as wildly as a guitar strum

When I wrote 'Survivor of the Auto da Fé' I had not read the Spanish poet Federico García Lorca, nor did I know anything about his fiery championship of *duende*.

Lorca's *duende* (in Andalusian Spanish it literally means a type of goblin) is impossible to summarise glibly. He originally presented his theory of the *duende* in an extraordinary public lecture in Cuba. *Duende* was the 'dark sounds' in art, especially in the performance of poetry, flamenco or bull-fighting. It was 'a duel with death'. I have always understood *duende* as working without a net, a soul-crunching risk, whether in the last poems of Sylvia Plath ('Lady Lazarus' and 'Daddy' are both superb examples) or in Maria Callas' recording of *Carmen* (she never performed the role on stage) when she draws the ace of spades and her voice is all dark chill, like grave dirt.

Lorca offers many fabulous examples himself, stressing that *duende* has nothing to do with mere technique or artifice. *Duende* is primitive and scary; it can make an audience weep or tear their clothes. The artist tumbles into dark peril— Lorca's own example is of a singer who horribly tears her voice to deliver the *duende* of the song. Lorca also uses *duende* as a measure. A work of art either has *duende* or it hasn't. An artist either has *duende* or hasn't. Weirdly, even though an exact meaning for *duende* will always remain elusive, whenever I have discussed or taught Lorca's famous *duende* lecture, everyone seems to recognise instantly what *duende* is—and rush up with their own examples.

When I wrote 'I burnt as wildly / as a guitar strum' in 'Survivor of the Auto da Fé', I was particularly inspired by a book I had accidentally stumbled upon, the pages of which were scorched with *duende*: *The Brothers Karamazov* by Fyodor Dostoyevsky. Just recently I have re-read the passage that poured into my seventeen-year-old imagination like fire water: 'The Grand Inquisitor', the unwritten poem by one of the Karamazov brothers, Ivan.

Jesus returns during the darkest days of the Spanish Inquisition and confronts the repellent ninety-year-old Grand Inquisitor, extreme old age at its most righteous and withered, framed in the stench of his latest mass auto-da-fé. I loved the broiling mix of devil's advocacy, melodrama, the eerie puzzle of faith and blackening human history. I loved Ivan's explanation of it as a sketch for a poem. And then I wrote my own. Was reading Dostoyevsky for the first time, gliding into the slipstream of his *duende*, the deepest inspiration for my poem? Was it more important than my own emotional maelstrom or the wild music I was imbibing at the time?

Has, in fact, reading been the greatest passion of my life? Are books more important to me than music, sex, nature, love— or writing itself?

Of course books can be just soft old slippers to slip into on a cold nasty night, comforters, reliable ports in a storm. But at a more profound level I recognise that there is something very unsettling about a book. Uncanny. A book written by a dead author—and most are (indeed there will come a time when I'm a dead author myself)—is nothing less than a haunted house, which lures the reader into conversation with a loquacious, enchanting ghost. We forget how mysterious, verging on the supernatural, reading is.

When I was four, my best friend was a fictional character—AA Milne's Christopher Robin. On a holiday with my parents and younger sister in the Blue Mountains, I spent much of it in play and silent communion with this hypnotising, imaginary, floppy-haired boy in the freezing shadow of giant pine trees. When something, maybe as benign as the intrusion of one of my parents, broke the spell I felt a terrible desolating loneliness that I can still remember.

In my collection *Crete*, there is a poem, 'The Dead', which describes my entranced unease about books:

Are our most violent poltergeists
books?

gnashing their shelves
smashing things in the dark

they leave a greenish tombish
smell on our reading fingers

they make us musty
and bereft.

These lines seem like a savage ingratitude
from a lifelong reading addict. Perhaps
what underlies them is my own fear of
the haunted house that my own work will
be—if it survives at all. Am I frightened
of the ghost I will become, trapped in my
own pages until, released by an unsuspect-
ing reader, I intone the same words over

and over again, like the phantom of Anne Boleyn carrying her head endlessly up and down the stairs of a famously haunted castle in England? How claustrophobic an obsession with immortality can be.

As I write and conclude this essay I am listening to a *saeta*—one of the *cante jondo* (deep song) forms of raw flamenco singing beloved by Lorca, which are sung without accompaniment. The word *saeta* means 'arrow', a song directed at the heavens. *Saetas* are performed during Holy Week in Spain, and are sung along the route of the procession to describe the sufferings of Christ, the torments of the Crucifixion and the sorrows of the Blessed Virgin. The voice of the *saeta* is a cry from a hard place, albeit a sacred one. A *saeta* is just one lone human voice, yet it hushes the crowd and creates a thrilling dread. It transcends the mortality, even the identity, of the singer. I've changed my heretic's mind about burning like a guitar strum. Far better for him or her or me to rise with the smoke on the flying arrow of the unaccompanied, unconfined voice. Fiery. Fabulous. Then gone.

Bibliography

Brontë, Emily, *Wuthering Heights and Poems*, JM Dent & Sons, Everyman's Library, Melbourne, 1987.

Cavafy, Constantine Petrou, *The Complete Poems of Cavafy*, translated by Rae Dalven, Harcourt Brace Jovanovich, New York, 1976.

——*The Essential Cavafy*, translated by Edmund Keeley and Philip Sherrard, The Ecco Press, New Jersey, 1995.

Donne, John, *John Donne: A Selection of His Poetry*, edited by John Hayward, Penguin Books, Ringwood, Australia, 1969.

Dostoyevsky, Fyodor, *The Brothers Karamazov,* Penguin Books, Ringwood, Australia, 1972.

Euripides, *The Bacchae and Other Plays,* Penguin Books, Ringwood, Australia, 1974.

García Lorca, Federico, 'Theory and Play of the *Duende*', viewed November 2009, <http://poetryintranslation.com/PITBR/Spanish/LorcaDuende.htm>.

Ginsberg, Allen, *Selected Poems 1947–1995*, Penguin Books, Camberwell, Australia, 2001.

Hopkins, Gerard Manley, *Poems and Prose*, edited by WH Gardner, Penguin Books, Ringwood, Australia, 1968.

Lawrence, DH, *D. H. Lawrence: Complete Poems*, Penguin Books, Ringwood, Australia, 1993.

Nietzsche, Friedrich, *The Birth of Tragedy and The Genealogy of Morals*, Doubleday Anchor, New York, 1956.

Paglia, Camille, *Sexual Personae*, Penguin Books, Ringwood, Australia, 1991.

——*Vamps and Tramps*, Vintage, New York, 1994.

——*Break Blow Burn*, Vintage, New York, 2005.

Porter, Dorothy, *Little Hoodlum*, Prism, Sydney, 1975.

——*Crete*, Hyland House, Melbourne, 1996.

Rimbaud, Arthur, *Rimbaud: Complete Works, Selected Letters*, translated by Wallace Fowlie, University of Chicago Press, Chicago, 1975.

Sappho, *Sappho*, translated by Mary Barnard, Shambhala Pocket Classic, Boston and London, 1994.

Shakespeare, William, *King Lear* in *The Complete Works of William Shakespeare, Volume 1, Tragedies and Poems*, William Collins, Sons & Co., London and Glasgow, 1964.

Permissions